The Young Girls Empowerment Manual

the leading young ladies

A basic guide for the young girls of our future.

Written By Elizabeth Pickens

"Do not let anyone ·treat you as if you are unimportant [despise/disregard/look down on you] because you are young. Instead, be an example to everyone with your words, your actions [conduct; behavior], your love, your ·faith [faithfulness], and your pure life."- 1 Timothy 4:12

This book is dedicated to Jada, Shanaya and Isabella.

"Do not just reach for the stars,
reach beyond them, and then you
will know what it feels like to touch Heaven."

Love,

Auntie Elizabeth

Embracing Your Beauty

As you grow older, you will learn that there are many other girls that are just like you. Some short, some tall, some with long hair, and others with short hair with different races and backgrounds of the like. However, there is only one YOU. You are Gods perfect gift to this entire world! When he made you, he took his time to form you into the perfect image and likeness of him. You are so special and unique that he took his time placing each and every strand of hair on your head. You are a wonderful creation, full of beauty and creativity!

All of Gods work is beautiful, just as you are. Nothing that he creates is ugly, unattractive or unappealing. My darling, everything about you is beautiful, and there is nothing at all wrong with you!

My Skin is Beautiful

Embrace the skin you are in. God loves a variety of colors and the color of your skin is a one of a kind. Your skin was mixed with just the right tones with a dash of SPARKLE!

My Face is Radiant

Your face has its own perfect shape with very special features. Your face represents your own special identity and was crafted perfectly by Gods hands just so people could tell who you are.

My Voice is Captivating

Your sound whether through sign language or audibly captivates all who encounter you. You have a voice to lead and to give hope to others.

My Body is Fabulous

You were created with your own unique shape. Shaped to perfection and made by the best hands. Your shape is beautiful and admiring to God.

" I am beautiful, I am fearfully and wonderfully made. God made no mistake when he made me because he made me to look like him. "

What do you love about yourself?

I love my: hair, body, and my personality. I like these things because they are apart of me and they help me embrace myself in the good and the bad.

I praise [thank] you because you made me in an amazing [awesome] and wonderful way. What you have done is wonderful. I know this very well.- Psalm 139:14

My darling, everything about you is beautiful, and ·there is nothing at all wrong with you [you have no blemish]-Song of Songs 4:7

Friendship

Friendships are a wonderful way to create a special bond with others while creating lasting memories. Everyone needs a friend to share their secrets with, to tell their jokes to, to share their accomplishments with and even for a shoulder to cry on.

In order to have a great friend, you must be a great friend. It starts with you treating others, how you would want to be treated. Would you want someone to make fun of you, or say mean things about you or spread rumors about you? Of course not! Good friends don't hurt each other's feelings, but instead, they love each other and learn to care for each other's feelings more than their own.

Being A Good Friend

Good Friends:

Love one another

Listens to one another

Communicates with each other

Shares with each other

Supports each other

Helps each other

Shows friendly affection through hugs

Is honest with one another

Good Friends Do Not:

Make fun of each other

Argue with each other

Become Jealous of one another

Does not share each other's secrets with others

Does not fight each other

Who is Your Best Friend?

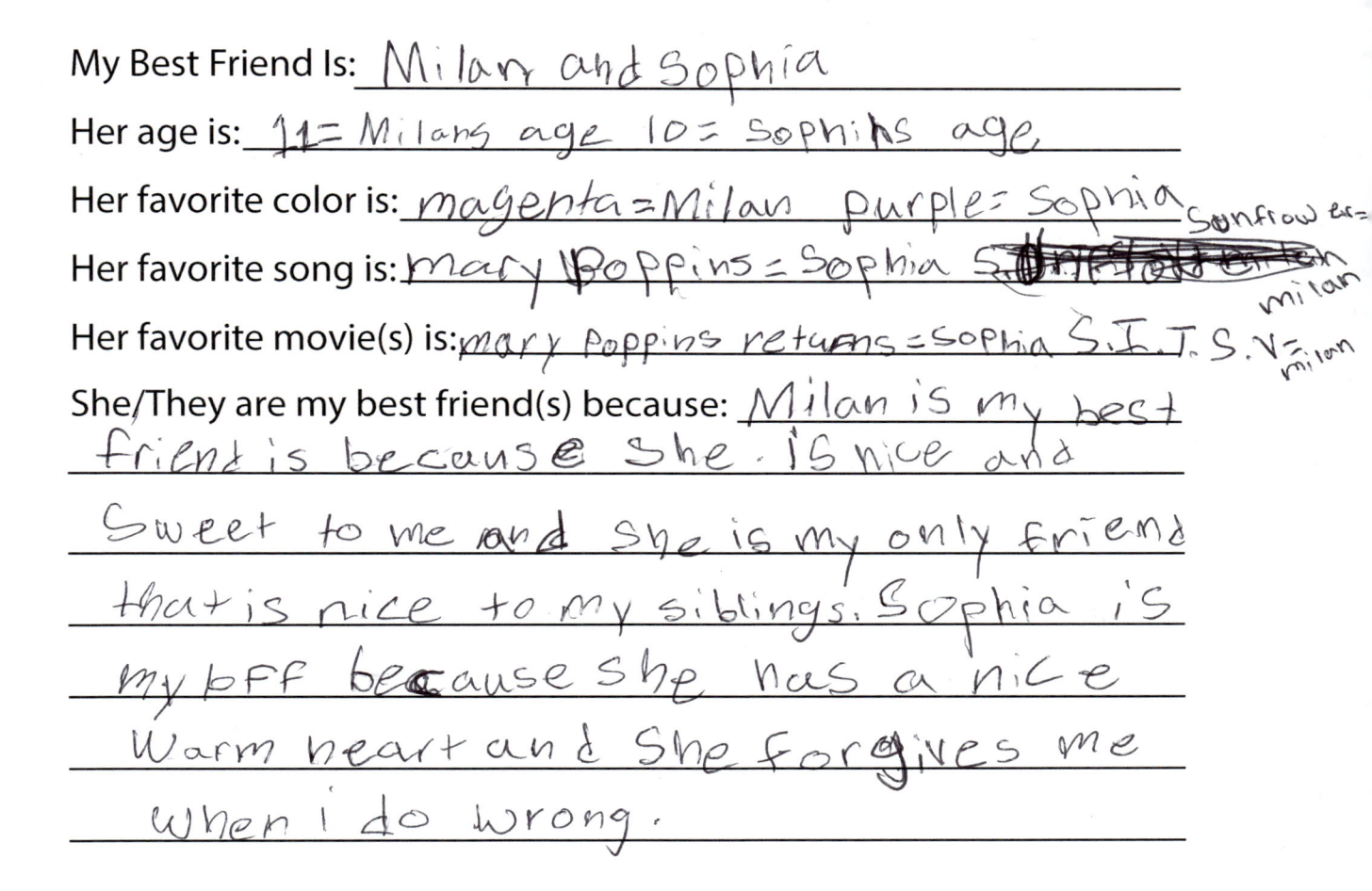

My Best Friend Is: Milan and Sophia

Her age is: 11= Milan's age 10= Sophia's age

Her favorite color is: magenta=Milan purple=Sophia sunflower=milan

Her favorite song is: Mary Poppins = Sophia ~~Sunflower~~ milan

Her favorite movie(s) is: Mary Poppins Returns = Sophia S.I.T.S.V = milan

She/They are my best friend(s) because: Milan is my best friend is because she is nice and sweet to me and she is my only friend that is nice to my siblings. Sophia is my bFF because she has a nice warm heart and she forgives me when I do wrong.

Do to others what [Treat others as] you would want them to ·do to [treat]you. Luke 6:31
Love [Be devoted to] each other ·like brothers and sisters [with family/brotherly affection]. ·Give each other more honor than you want for yourselves [or Outdo one another in showing honor; or Be eager to show honor to one another] Romans 12:10

Let us think about ·each other and help each other [or how to provoke/rouse/encourage each another] to show love and do good deeds. Hebrews 10:24

Bullying

Bullying hurts others and should never be tolerated. As a young lady, you should never join others to harass your peers. Actions like these only make matters worse and can lead to disciplinary action. Never join in bullying. If you see someone bullying others, immediately tell an authority that you trust but do not join in or try to handle the problem on your own.

Bullies often want an audience and approval by others. They want people to join in with their behavior and make people feel afraid of them. It is never okay to encourage bullying because it only hurts the one who is being bullied more.

Be the role model and lead by example in your school. Treat everyone fairly and be at peace with everyone. Surround yourself with positive people who get along with others rather than bully others. Do not be fooled, bad friends will ruin a good character, so make sure that you are hanging around others who are positive and not negative.

Have you been bullied before? YES/ NO

How did you feel when you were bullied?

It made me feel:

Yes I have been bullied before and it did not feel good. This was for two years. This was because my cousin would listen to her friends to stay away from me. I got so bad when I was in 3rd grade to where I had to fight to protect myself

If you have been bullied before, you should talk to someone to let them know how you currently feel. Talking to an authority, helps you to release any emotional feelings as well as put a plan of action in place in the event that someone trys to bully you again.

Are you being bullied now?

If you are being bullied now, the best thing that you should do is seek help from a parent/ guardian, teacher, principal, counselor or someone in authority. If someone has bullied you, do not repay them by doing wrong to them but instead, seek help immediately from someone in authority.

If someone does wrong to you, do not pay him back by doing wrong to him [Repay no one evil for evil]. Try to do [or Consider carefully] what everyone thinks is right [others view as good/honorable;is good/noble before all people]. Romans 12:17

Have you bullied someone?

If you have ever bullied someone, consider how you would feel if someone did to you, what you did to them. Bullying is never okay and should not be taken as a joke. If you have offended someone, it is always wise to go to that person and apologize. Your actions and words have a major impact on others.

Ways to apologize

Write a letter
Have a conversation and offer an apology
Have lunch with them

Steps to Stop Bullying

SPEAK UP and STAND UP for yourself. Express to the person that you do not appreciate the way that you are being treated. A gentle [soft; tender] answer ·will calm a person's anger, but an ·unkind answer ·will cause more anger. Never respond out of fear or anger. Immediately tell and adult. If the individual continues to bully you, tell an adult.

Stay away from bullies. Stay away from those who are bullies as well as those who are friends with the bullies. Surround yourself with new friends or people who are nice and exemplify the character of a good friend.

Do not be ·fooled [deceived; misled]: "Bad ·friends [company] will ruin good ·habits [or character; morals; a quote from the Greek poet Menander." 1 Corinthians 15:33

If someone does wrong to you, do not pay him back by doing wrong to him [Repay no one evil for evil]. ·Try to do [or Consider carefully] what ·everyone thinks is right [others view as good/honorable; [is good/noble before all people]. Romans 12:17

A ·gentle [soft; tender] answer ·will calm a person's anger [turns back/away wrath], but an ·unkind [painful; sharp] answer ·will cause more [raises] anger. Proverbs 15:1

Emotions

Everyone is created with emotions. It is a natural way of how we express our feelings. Unfortunately, girls tend to express their feelings very different from boys. Our emotions are affected by what we see, hear, feel, touch and even smell. Girls tend to be more sensitive to these five senses. As a young lady, in order for you to control your emotions, you must learn to control what affects your senses. What affects your five senses usually affects your thoughts and out of your thoughts come the decisions and choices that you make in life.

As young ladies, we must choose wisely what we listen to, what we watch, who we hang around and even what we say because it affects our life and our emotions. Not all emotions are bad. Emotions such as being Happy or Joyful can come from positive moments and memories.

What makes you Happy?

Being around family and friends.

Other emotions such as being angry, sad or afraid can come from bad memories or moments.

What makes you angry?

We people get on my last nerves.

What makes you afraid?

When I have bad dreams.

I am strong, I am courageous. I am not afraid. Where ever I go, God is with me.

Remember that I [Have I not…?] commanded you to be strong and ·brave [courageous; resolute]. Don't be afraid or ·discouraged [dismayed], because the Lord your God will be with you ·everywhere you go [or in all you do]." Joshua 1:9

Be careful what you think [Above all that you guard, protect your heart], because · your thoughts run your life [life flows from it]. Proverbs 4:23

Hygiene

As a young lady, it is important that you keep up with your hygiene. Your hygiene is very important because it affects others that come around you. When you have bad odor, it keeps people from wanting to hang around you. Would you want to hang around someone who smelled like a sour trash can? Of course not! And besides, you are a young lady and young ladies always want to smell good and be presentable.

Steps to Maintaining a Healthy Hygiene

Take a shower/ bath every day

Brush your teeth and floss at least twice a day

Comb your hair every day

Change your under clothes every day

Iron your clothes before you wear them. (Never go out in public wrinkled)

Use gentle deodorants (ask your parents what deodorant is best for you)

It is also a good practice to keep the following in your purse:

Hand sanitizer
Travel tooth brush/ tooth paste
Kleenex
Mints
Lotion
Comb/Brush

For Girls Who Have Periods:

Take a shower/ bath every day while you are on your menstrual cycle (period). This will help eliminate the smell and relax your muscles which will minimize your cramps (if you have any). You also will want to make sure that your "lady parts" stay very clean to avoid any infections, which are no fun!

You should change your sanitary napkins (pads) at least every 3 to 4 hours to help keep your "lady parts clean" and to avoid rashes and irritations.

It is important that you make it a practice to keep in your purse sanitary napkins (pads), an extra pair of undies, and sanitary wipes (the non-scented kind) just in case you begin spotting while you are away from home.

Ask your parents about a safe medication such as Ibuprofen or Tylenol that you can take to alleviate cramps.

During this time, you will want to drink plenty of water to stay hydrated and *STAY AWAY FROM FRIED and UNHEALTHY FOODS.*

You should [Don't you...?] know that your body is a temple for the Holy Spirit who is in you and was given to you by God. 1 Corinthians 6:19

Boys!- Eww!

So you are at a time in your life were boys are starting to like you, and of course you probably like them back, right? Well of course you do! Liking the opposite sex (boys) is completely natural and okay. However, as young ladies, we must make sure that our actions are pure and that we are not being pressured into doing anything that God and our parents would not approve of.

If a boy likes you

Make sure that he respects your body, your boundaries and your space. It is never okay for a boy to touch you in any way other than hug. Never feel pressured to do anything that you do not want to do.

If a boy tries to pressure you into doing something that you are uncomfortable in doing, immediately tell a person of authority whether it be your teacher or your parents.

If you like a boy: It is okay to like him, but it is NOT okay for you to engage in bad activities that God or your parents would not approve of. It is okay to engage in casual conversations and even hang around him. But always be with a friend or a group of friends while you are interacting with him. Keep your hands to yourself. And never feel pressured by friends or by a boy to do something that you are not comfortable in doing. If there is a boy you like, it is always good to express your feelings of interest to your parents so you will know their expectations of you.

Parents and Authority

Your parents and authority were created to help you advance and grow in life. God gave you parents to love you, protect you, provide for you and raise you to be the best that you can be when you get older. Sometimes, it may feel like your parents are not treating you fairly, but let's be honest, they are older than you, bigger and a lot smarter than you and in the end, they only want to do what's best for you. You may not always agree with everything that they say or do, but it is a good practice to still obey and honor them. Obeying your parents means that you, listen when they ask you to do something, you never talk back when you disagree with what they are saying and you learn to submit to their request even if you do not agree with them. Honor means that you respect them at all times. You don't talk bad about them or say mean things at them. You show them that you appreciate them through your love and obedience towards them.

Different ways that I can obey my parents:

Making good grades
Keep my room clean
Be nice to my siblings, friends and family
Helping around the house
Helping my parents when asked
Being honest

Different ways that I can honor my parents:

Doing nice things for them
Telling them that I love them and appreciate what they do for me
Writing them a letter
Helping them with dinner
Keeping the house clean

]My child [son], listen to your father's ·teaching [instruction; discipline] and do not · forget [neglect] your mother's advice [instruction] For Their teaching [It] will be like ·flowers in your hair [a gracious garland on your head] or a necklace [beads] around your neck. Proverbs 1:8-9

Children, obey your parents ·as the Lord wants [in the Lord], because this is ·the right thing to do [right; just]. 2 The command says, "Honor your father and mother [Ex. 20:12; Deut. 5:16]." This is the first command that has a promise with it— 3 "Then everything will be well with you, and you will have a long life on the earth. Ephesians 6:1-3

Perfecting Your Craft, Skills, and Hobbies

Your skills are a perfect way to help others. You were created with a very special skill to share with this entire world! As young ladies, this is a good time to find something that you love to do. Whether it be singing, drawing, acting or dancing, this is an excellent time for you to practice your skill. You can do anything that you put your heart to. Never let anyone make you feel like you can't, because you CAN.

I can do anyhting that I put my mind to. I am strong, I am smart, and I am confident!

What are your favorite hobbies?

My favorite hobbies are...

Playing basketball, playing with my friends, siblings, and reading.

What is one thing that you would like to learn how to do?

I would like to learn how to...

Speak fluently in Spanish and manderin.

I can do all things through ·Christ, because he [the one who] gives me strength.
Philippians 4:13

7 Keys for Leading Little Ladies

Have Courage

Be Courageous in all that you do, because you've got girl power and you can do anything!

Do Not Fear

Do not be afraid to take chances or try new things. You were born to be fearless.

Be Kind

Be Kind to others always helping in whatever way that you can.

Be Consistent

Keep on trying. Don't stop because it gets hard, but keep pursuing your dreams until you can see them.

Lead by Example

Encourage others to do whats right by doing good to others and for others.

Believe in Yourself

There is no doubt that you are special and amazing in every way. You can do whatever your heart desires. Just believe.

Be Yourself

This world needs YOU! Give this world the best version of you!

Use your voice for kindness, your ears for compassion, your hands for charity, your mind for truth and your heart for Love." – Unknown

Notes

I should keep-up my hygiene. I should also be interactive with my peers and my family.

Made in the USA
Columbia, SC
01 March 2019